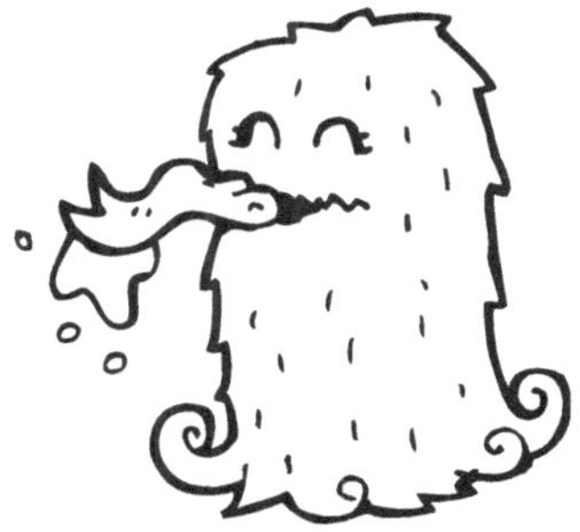

THIS MONSTER BOOK BELONG TO

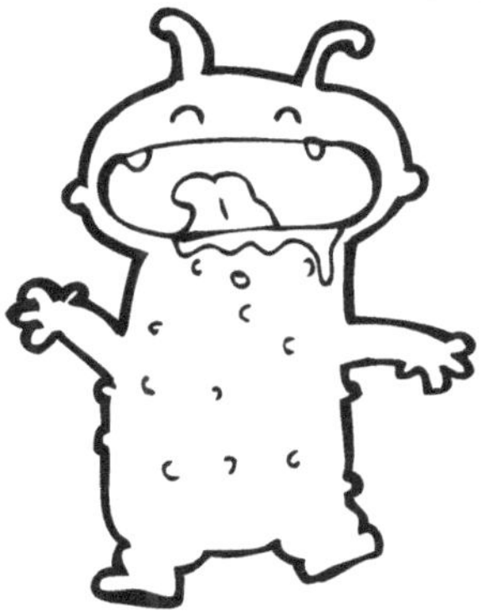

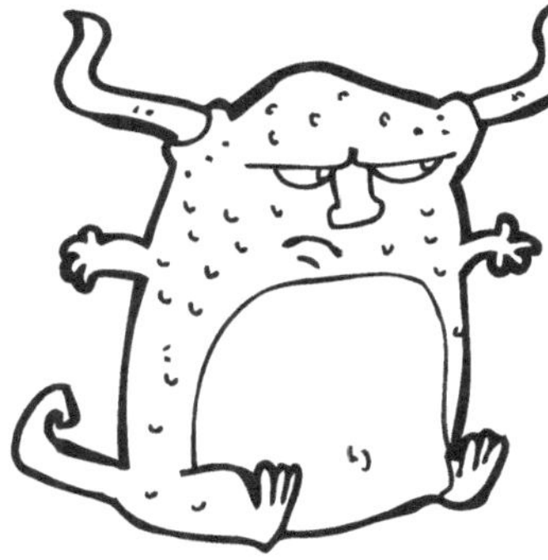

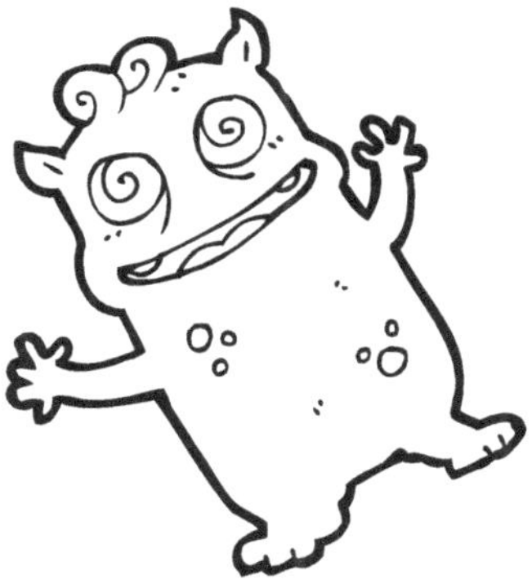

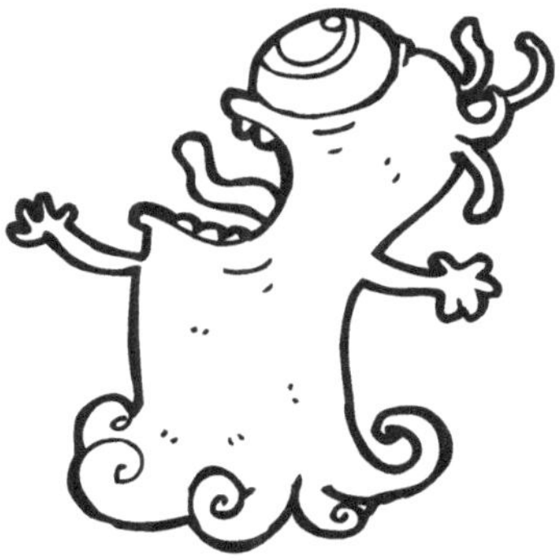

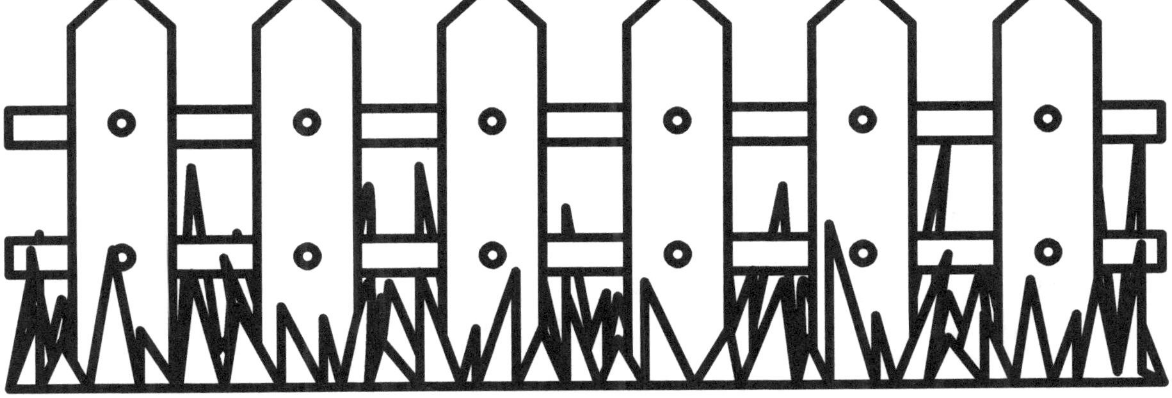

BY: MR PASQUALEE

AM I CUTE?

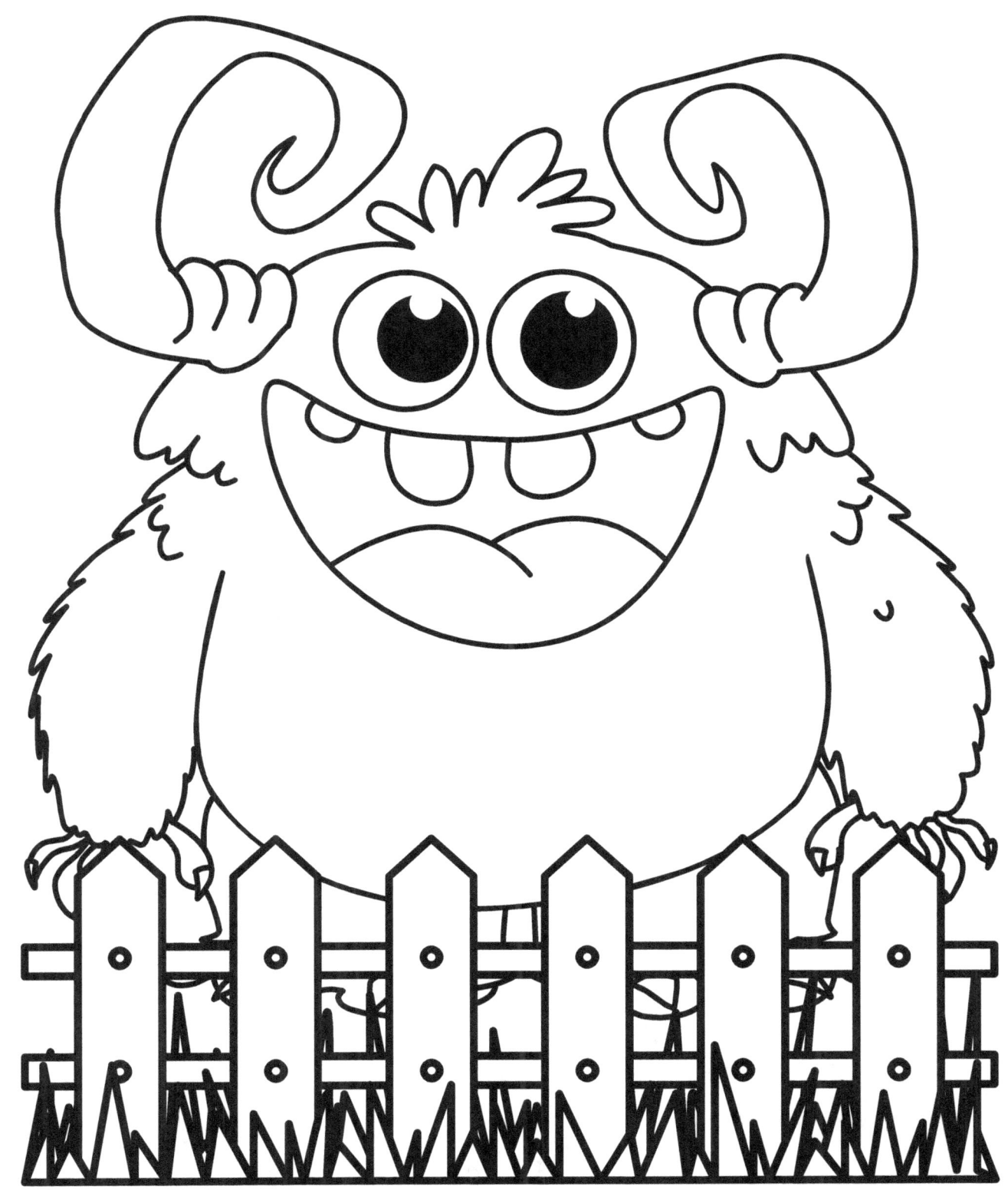

I AM HAPPY

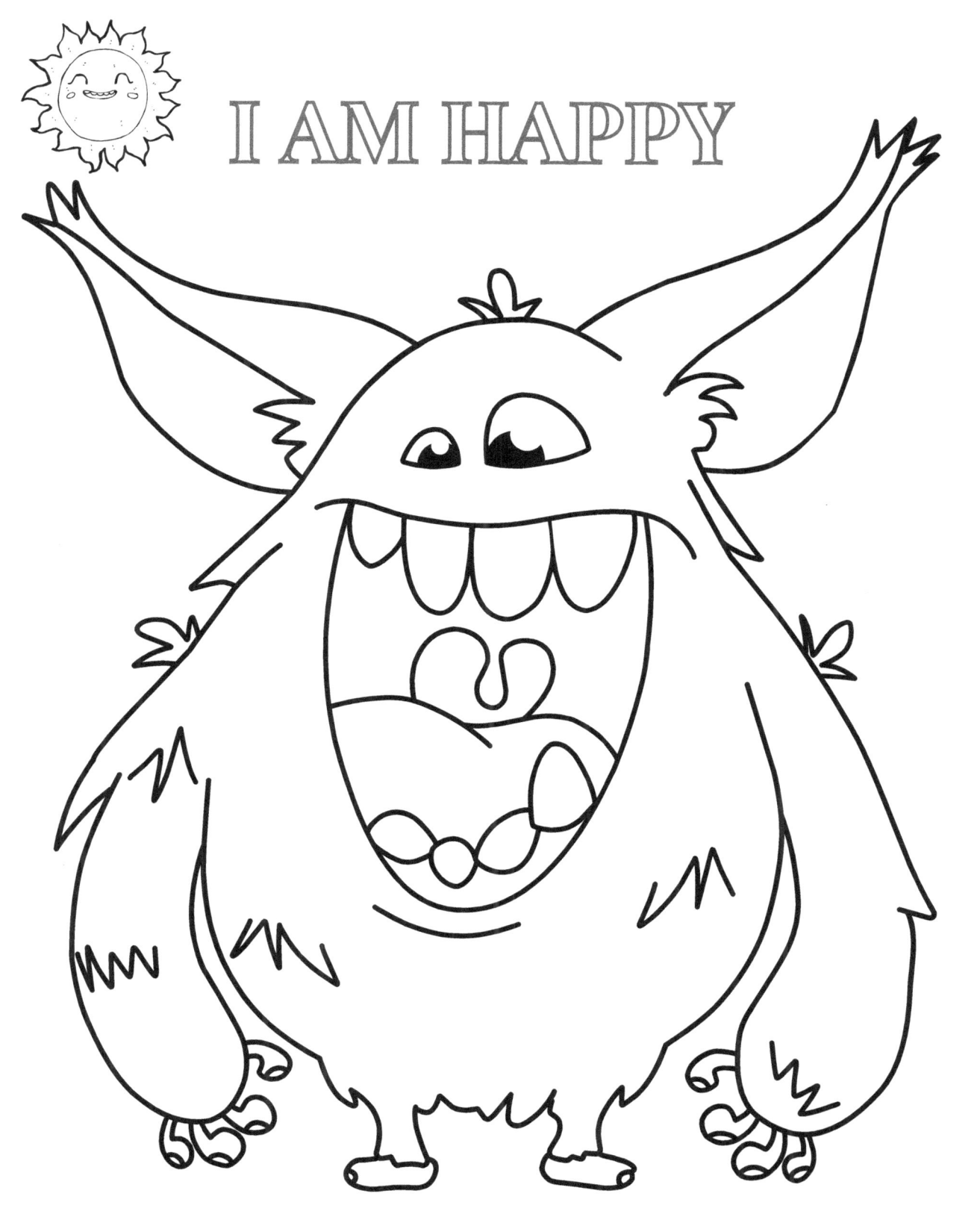

HELLO MY FRIEND

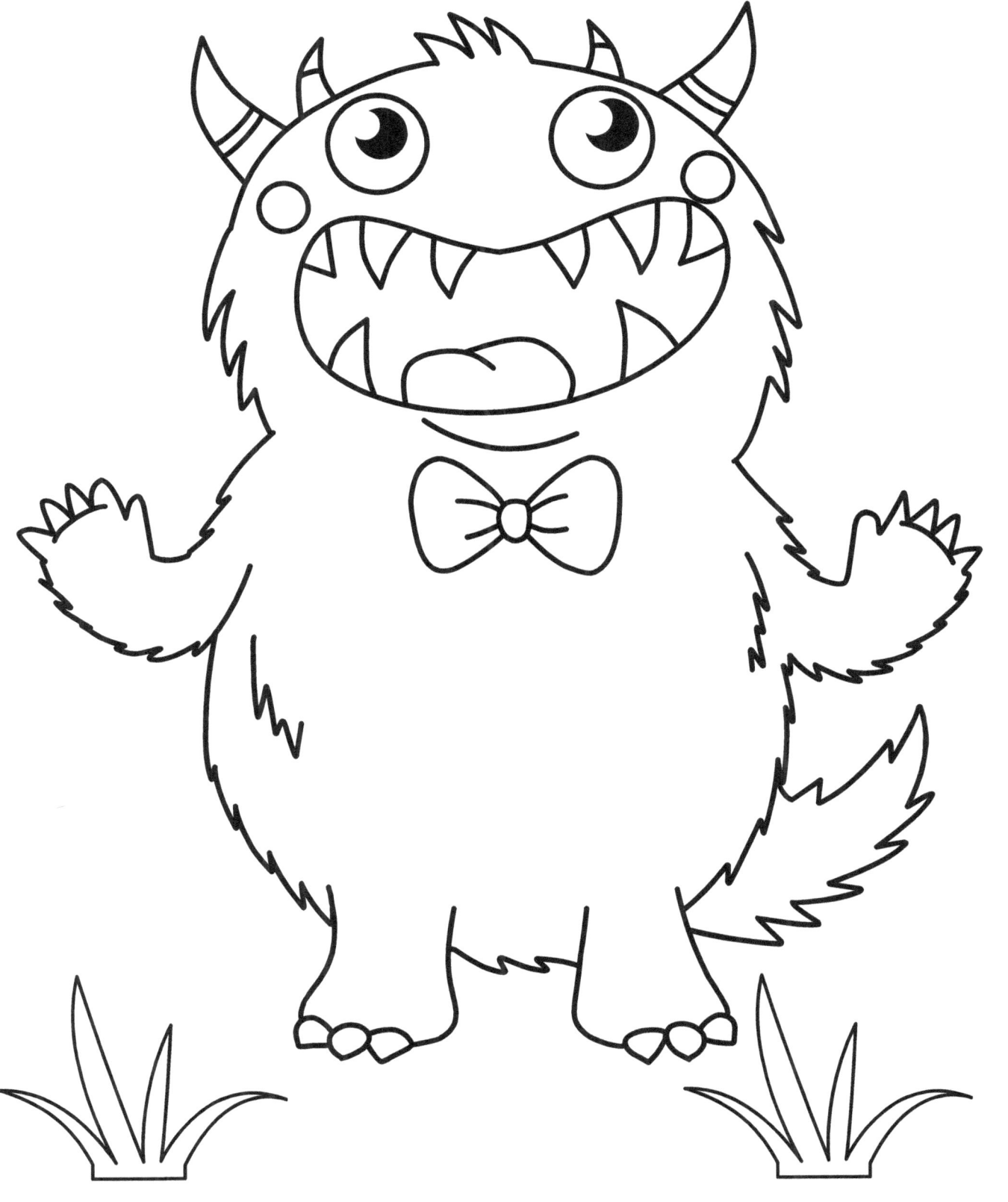

I CAN SEE YOU!

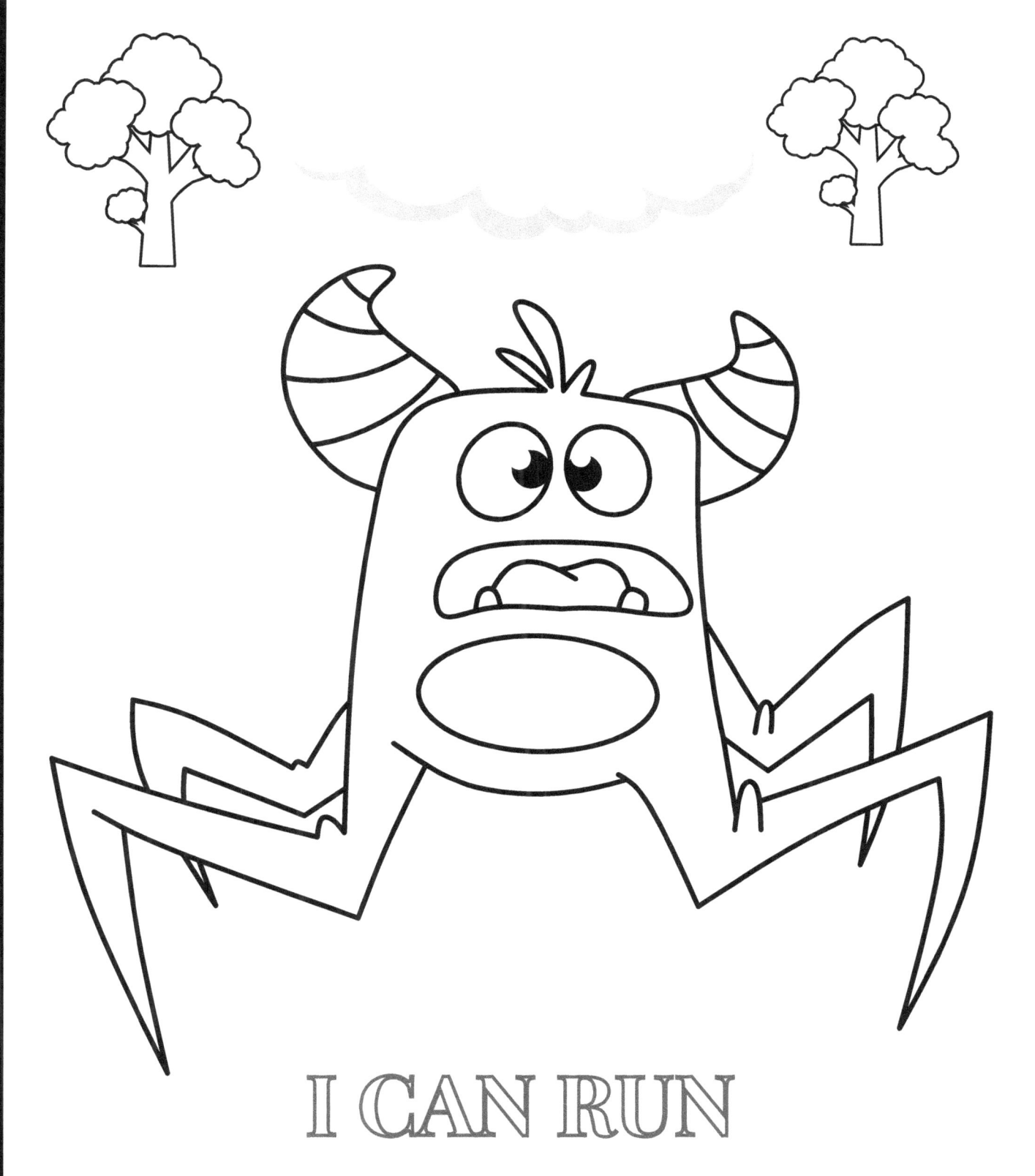

I AM VERY STRONG

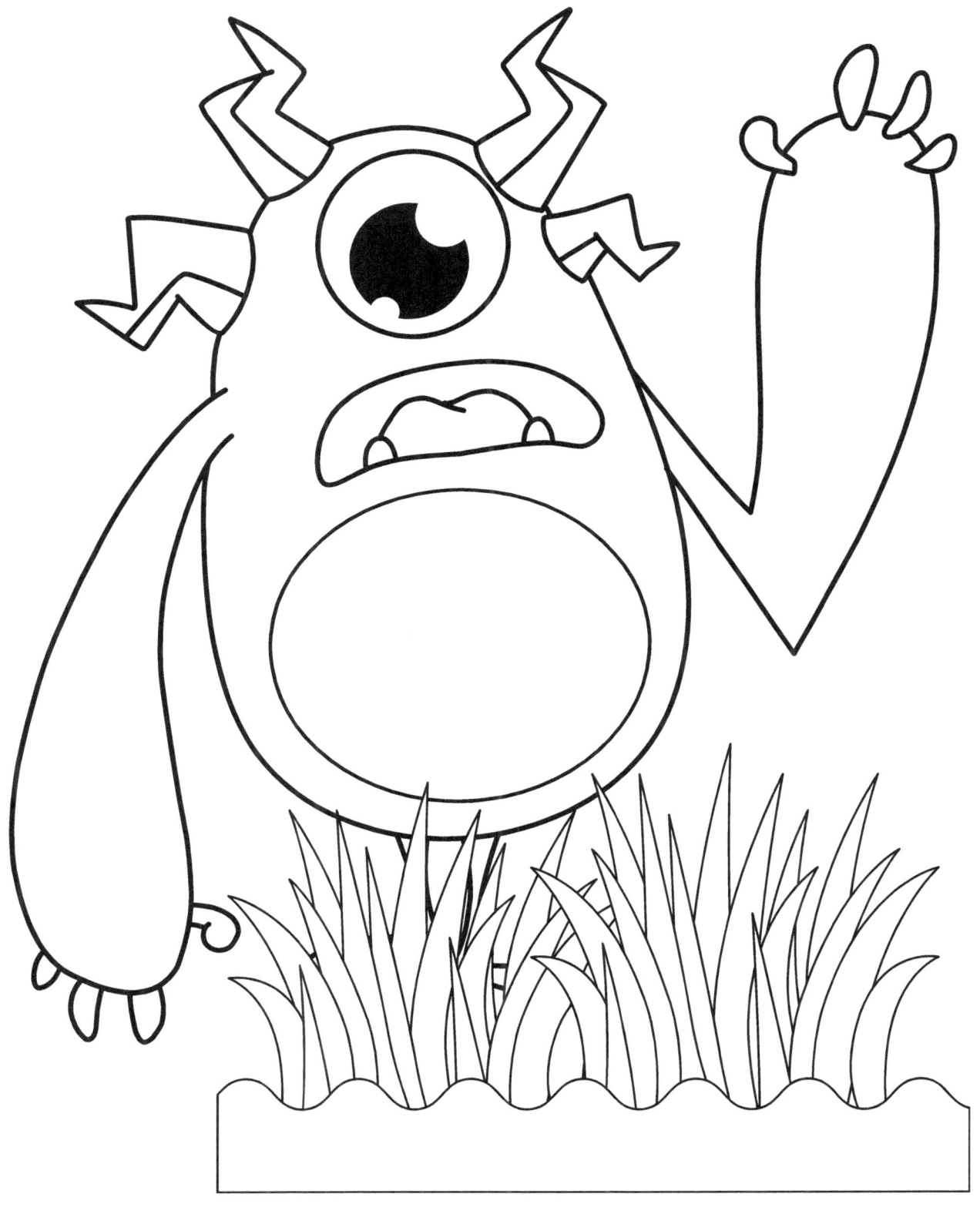

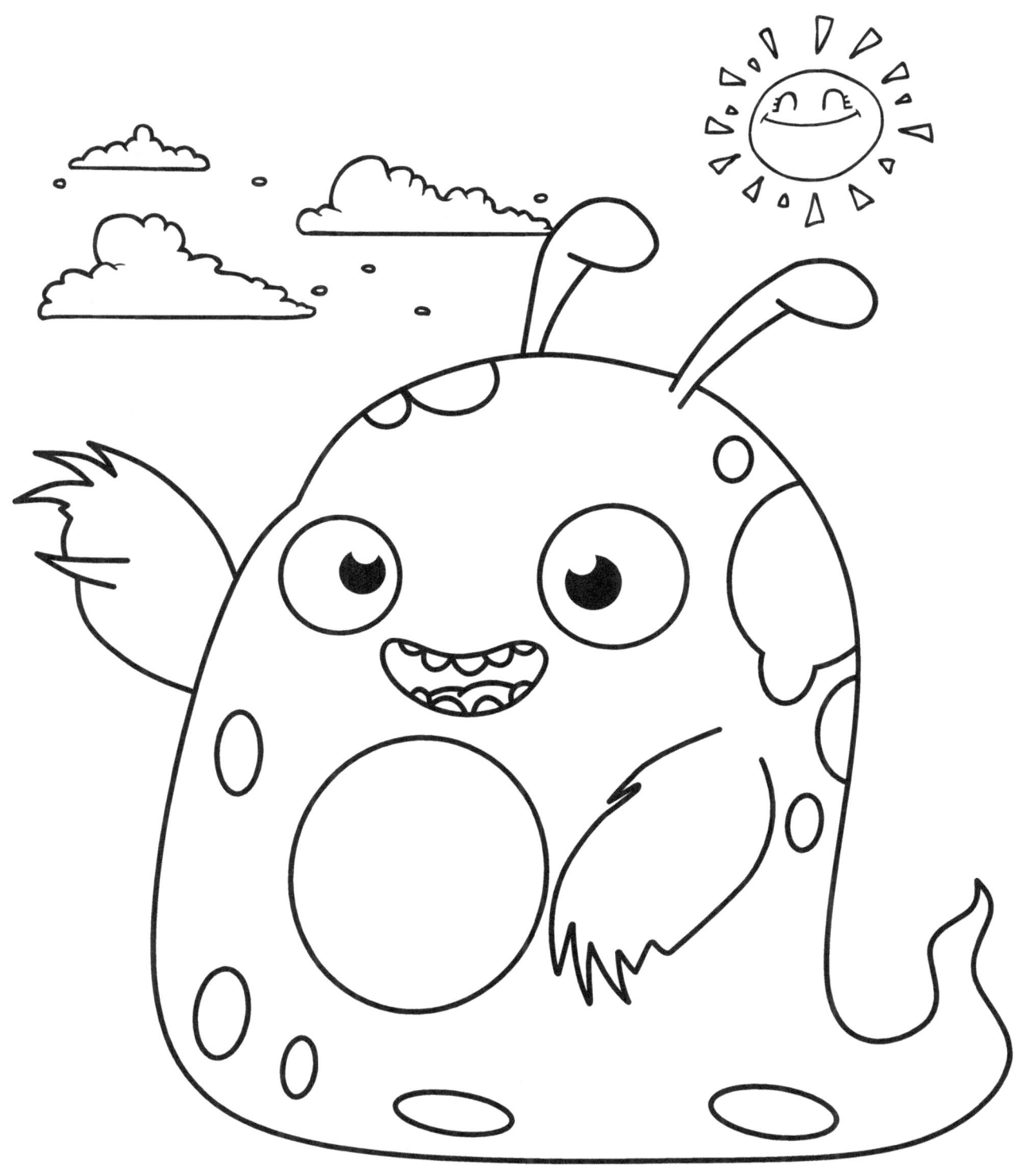

I AM VERY PROUD

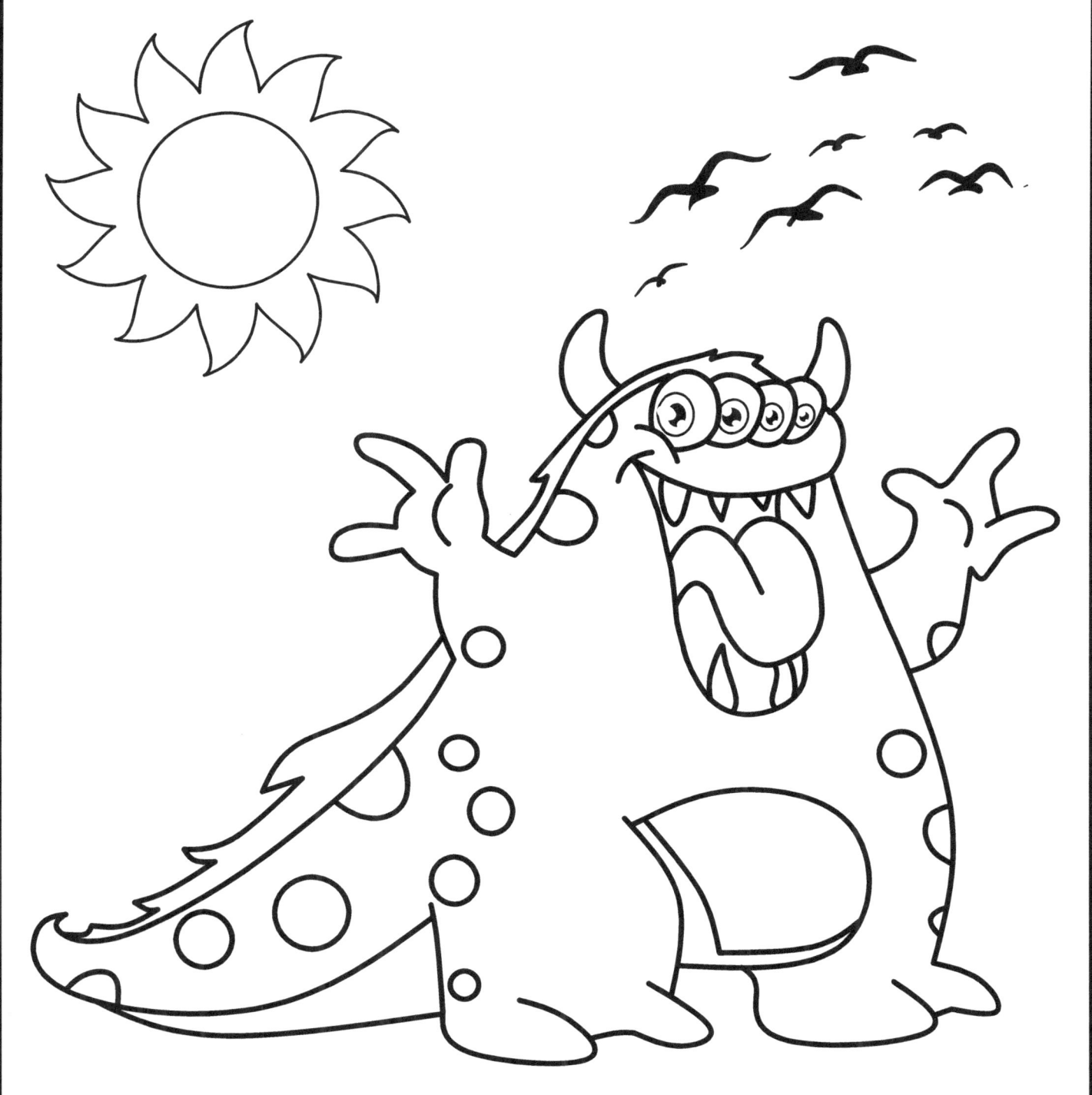

I CAN DANCE

IT IS LUNCH TIME

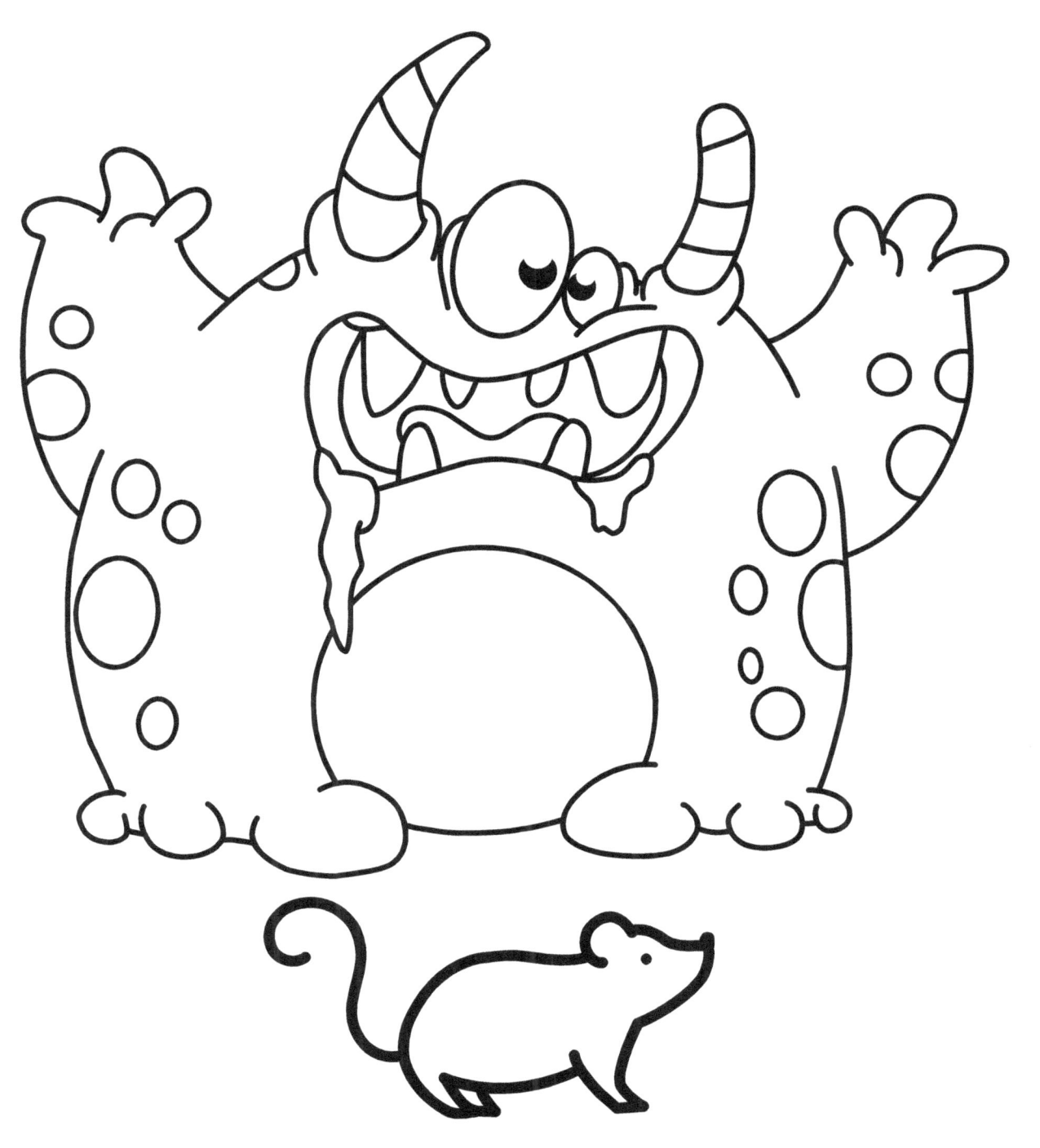

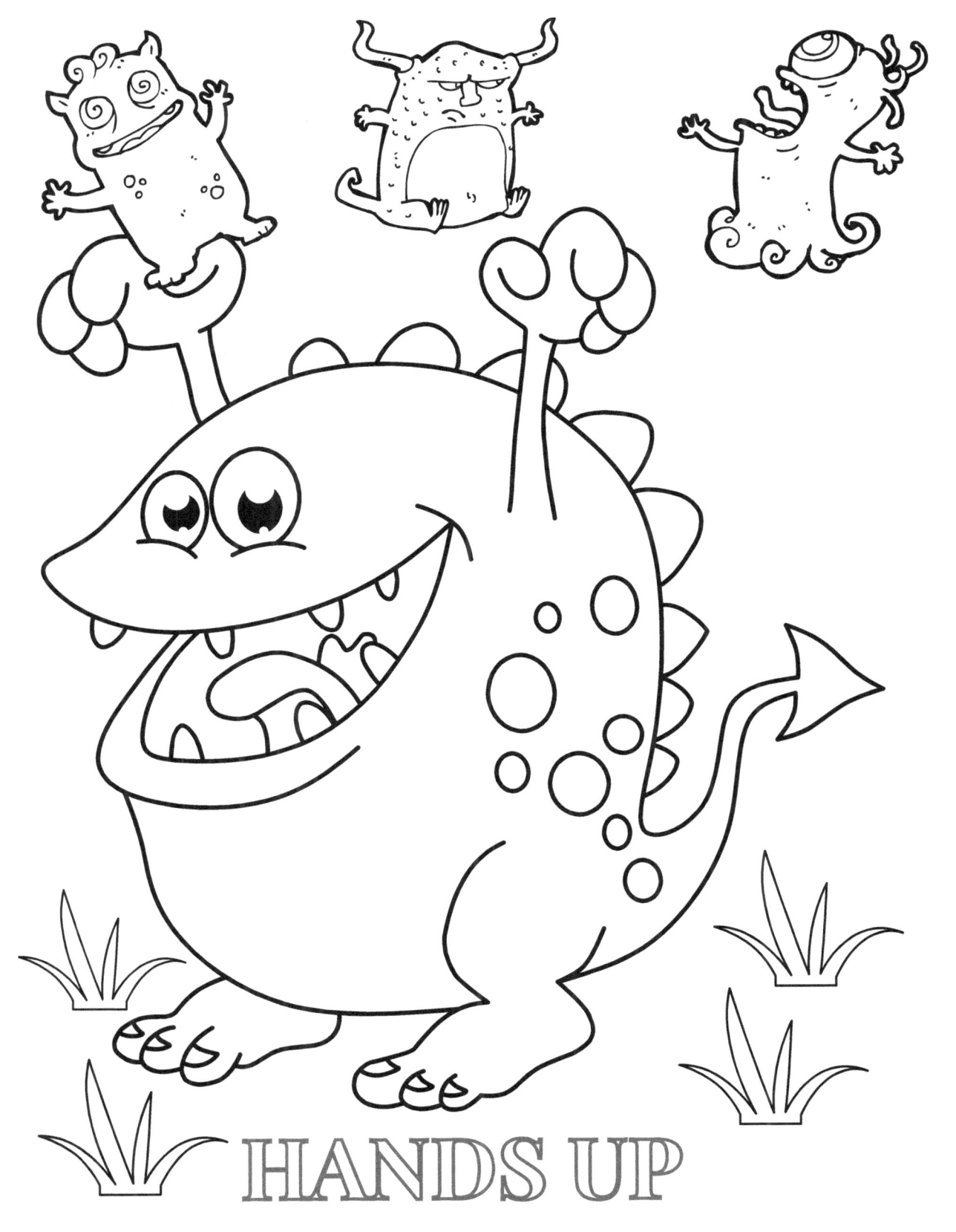

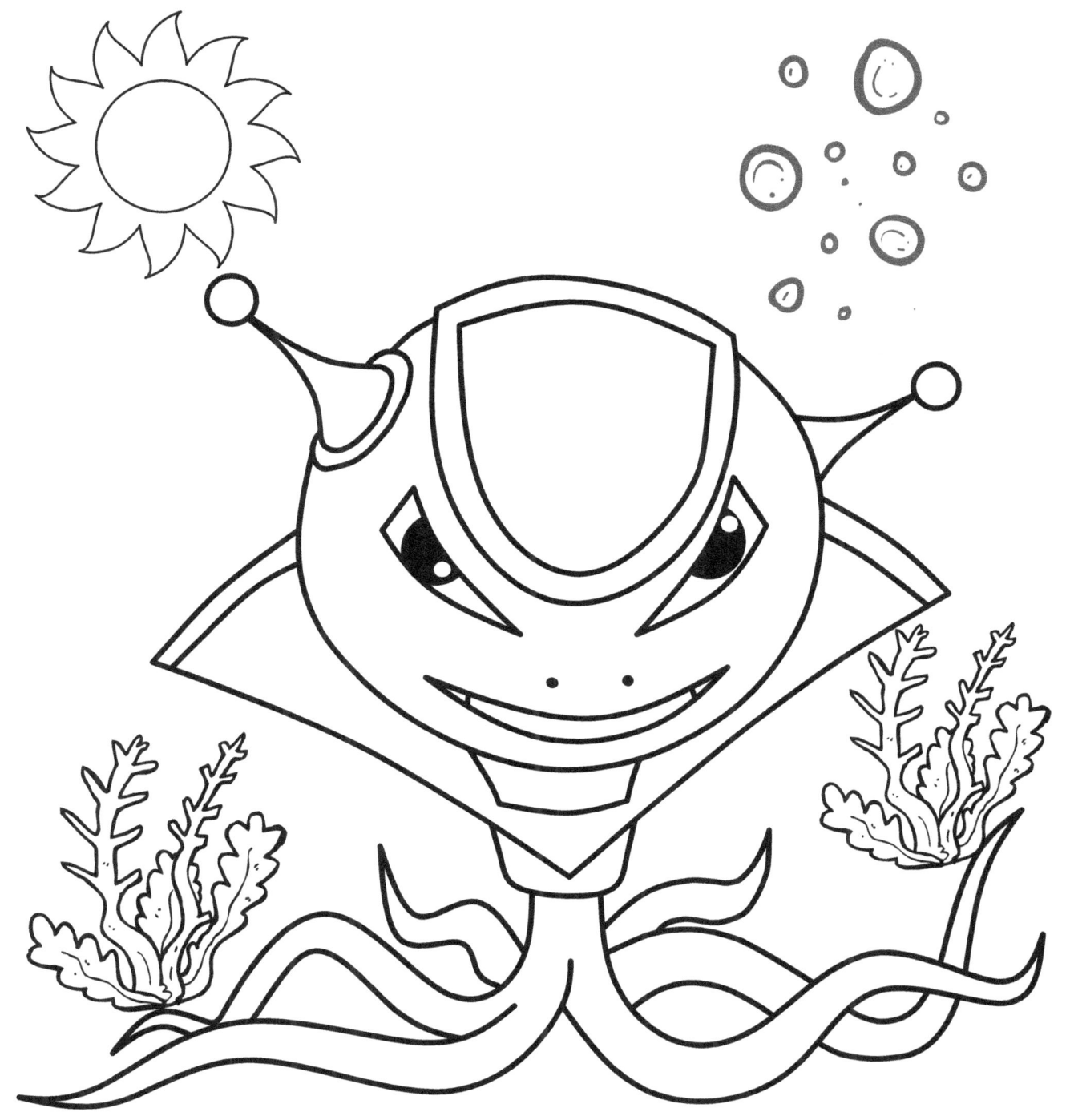

IT IS A SUNNY DAY

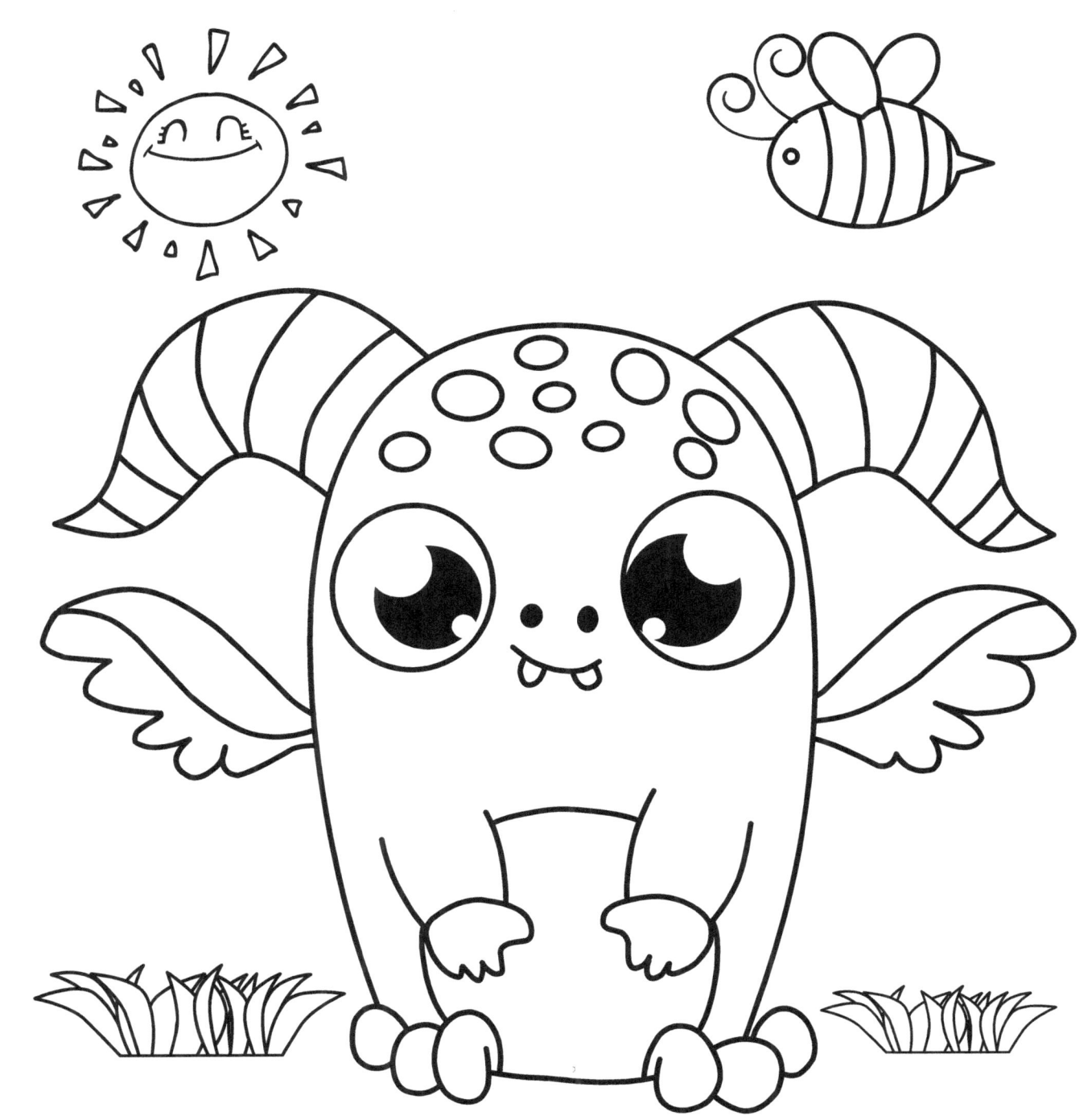

I HAVE BIG EARS

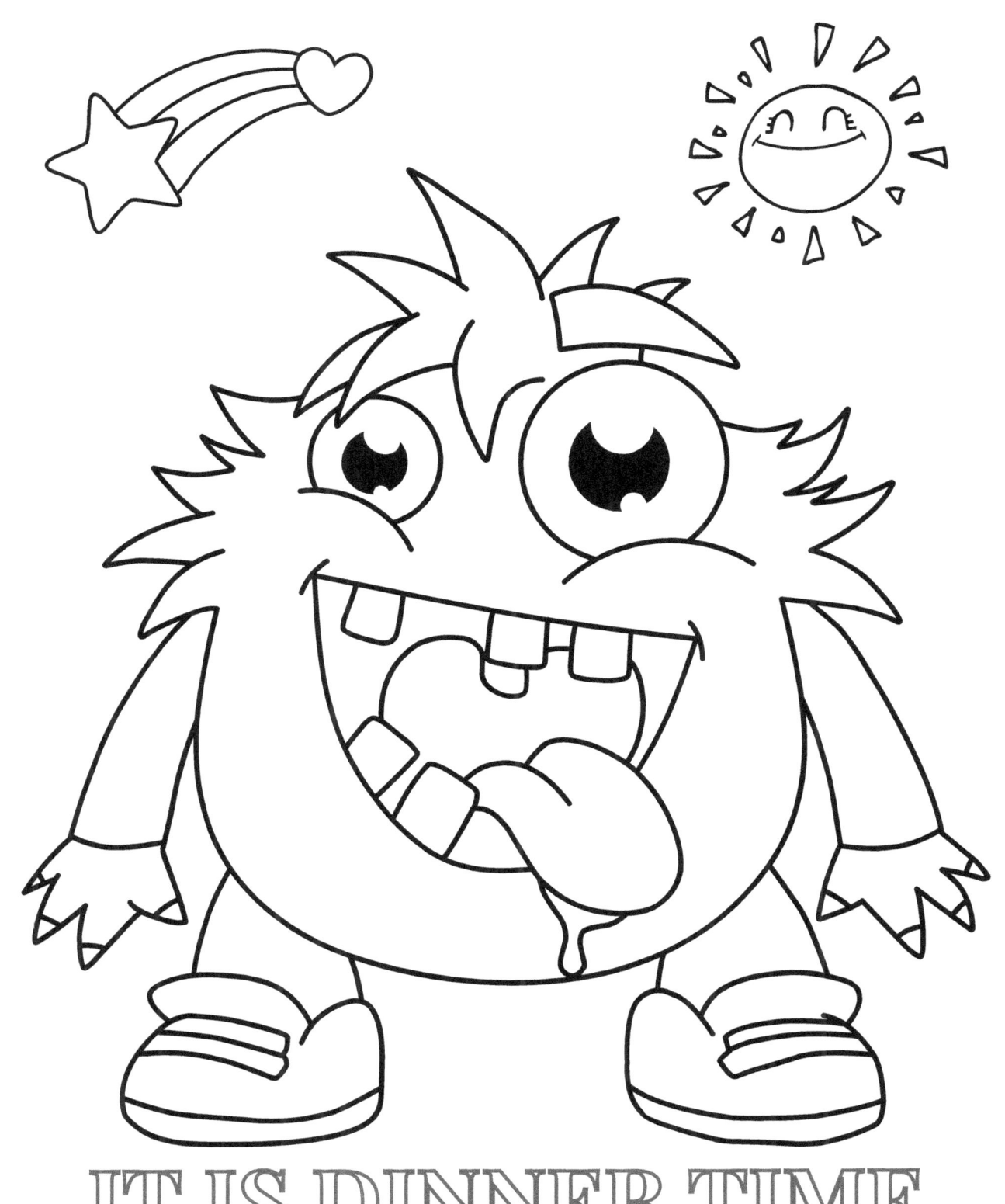

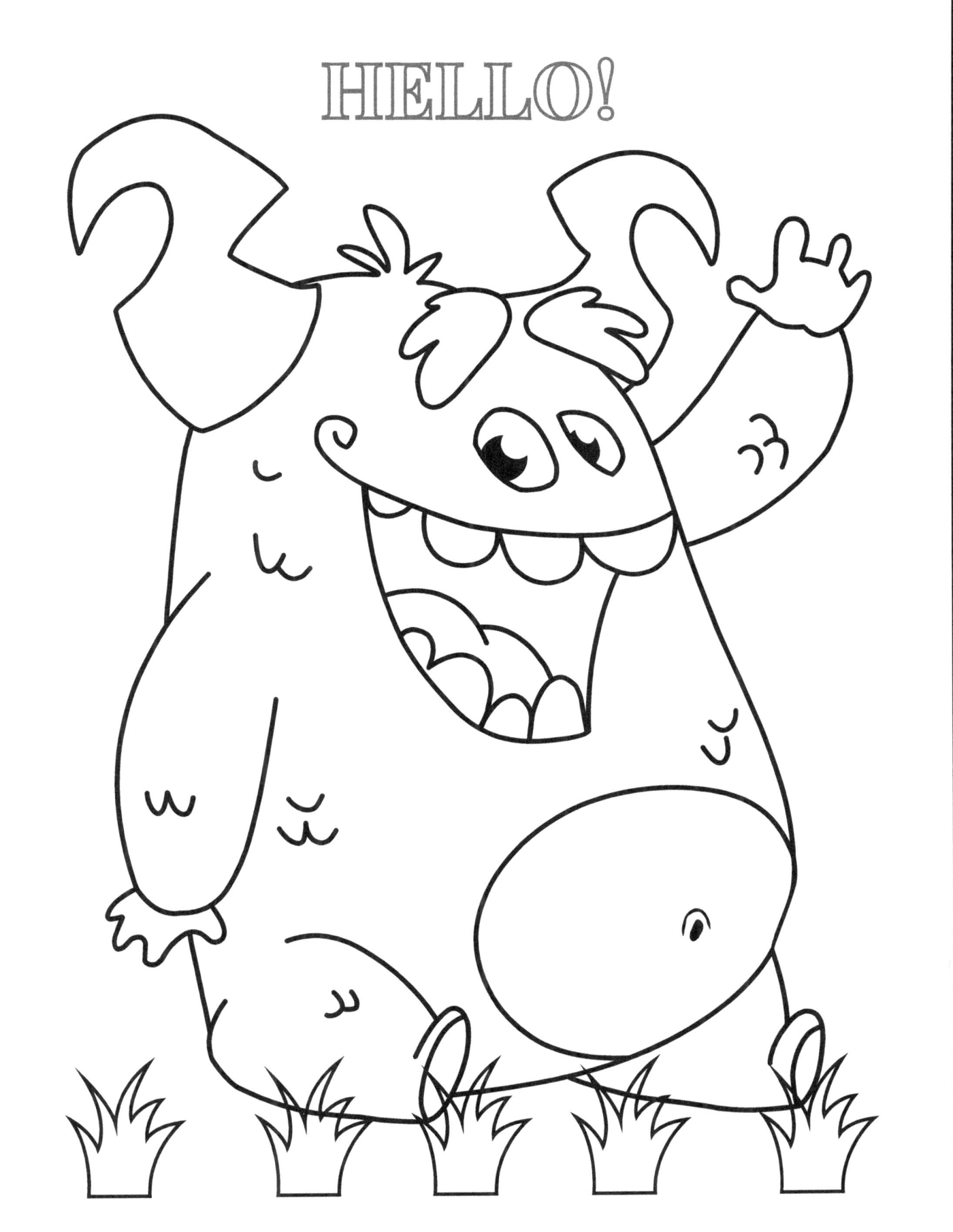

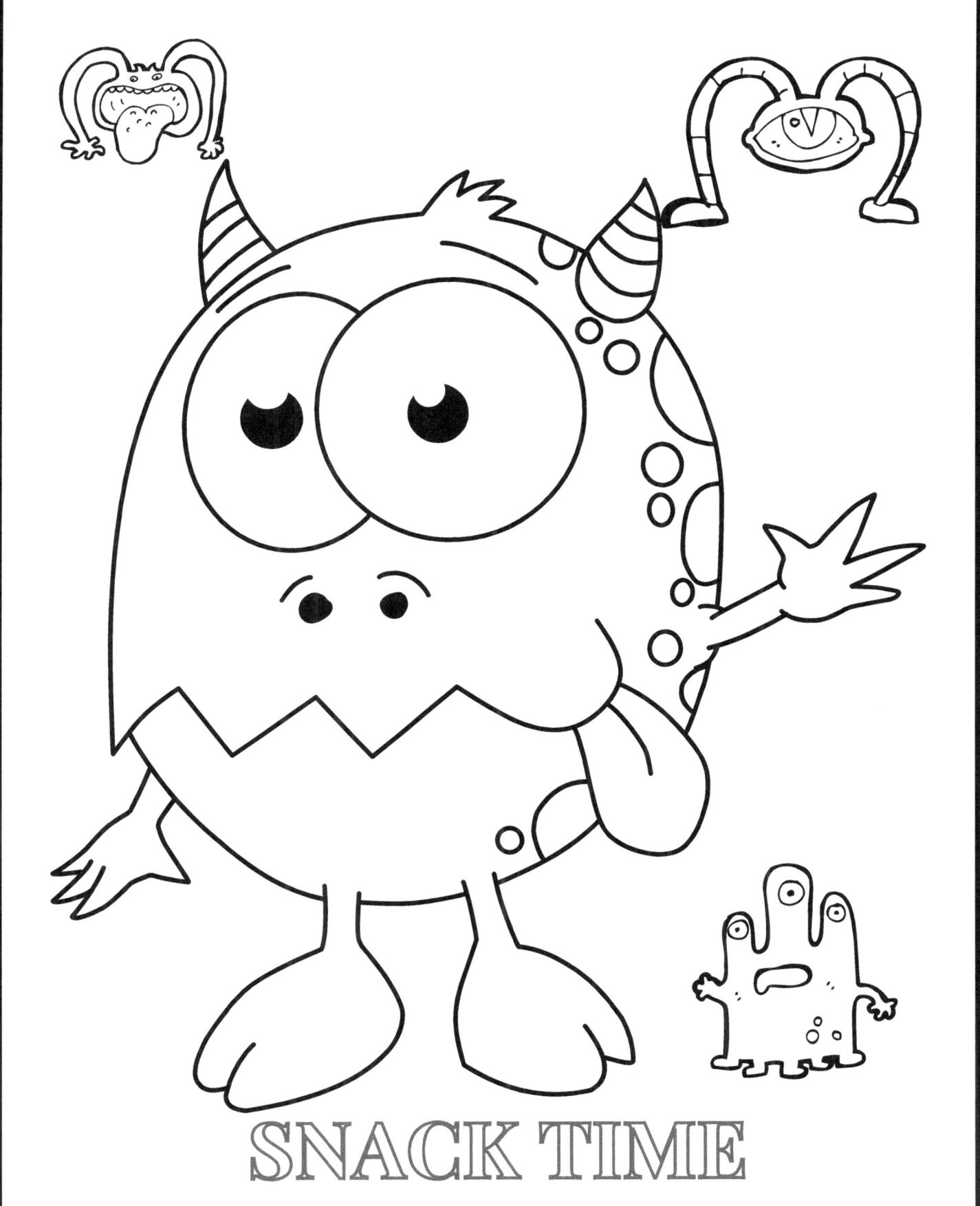

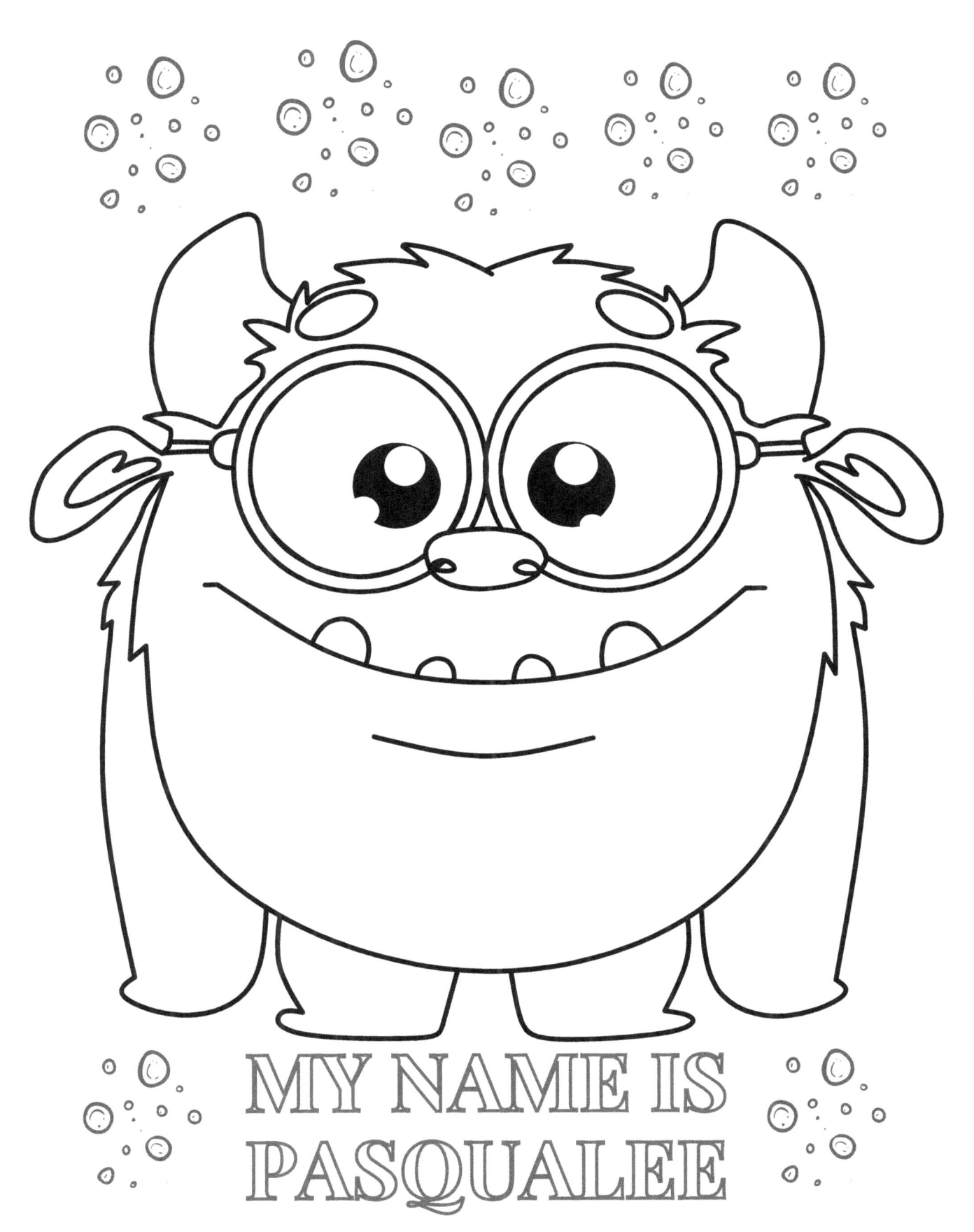

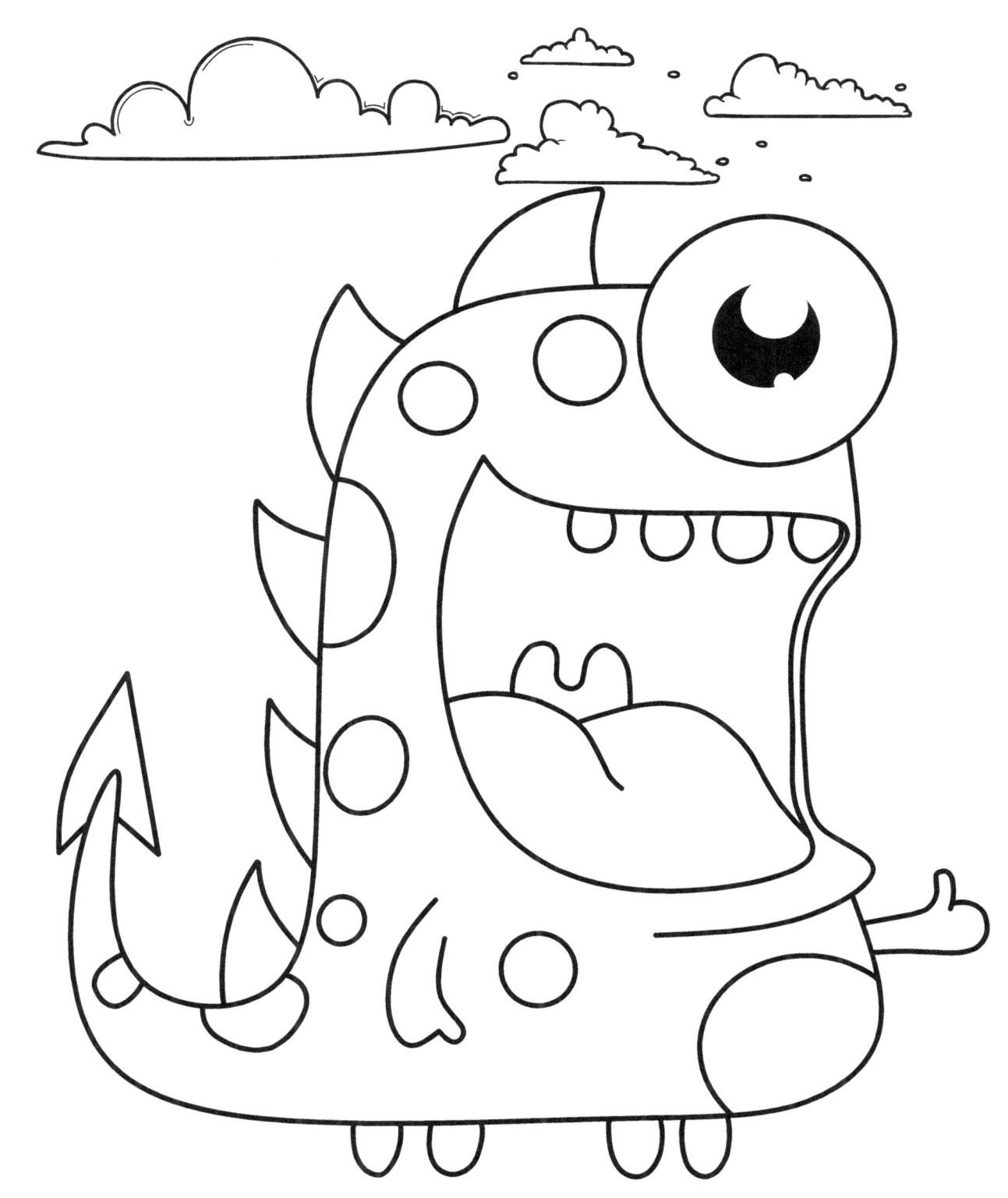

IT IS A CLOUDY DAY

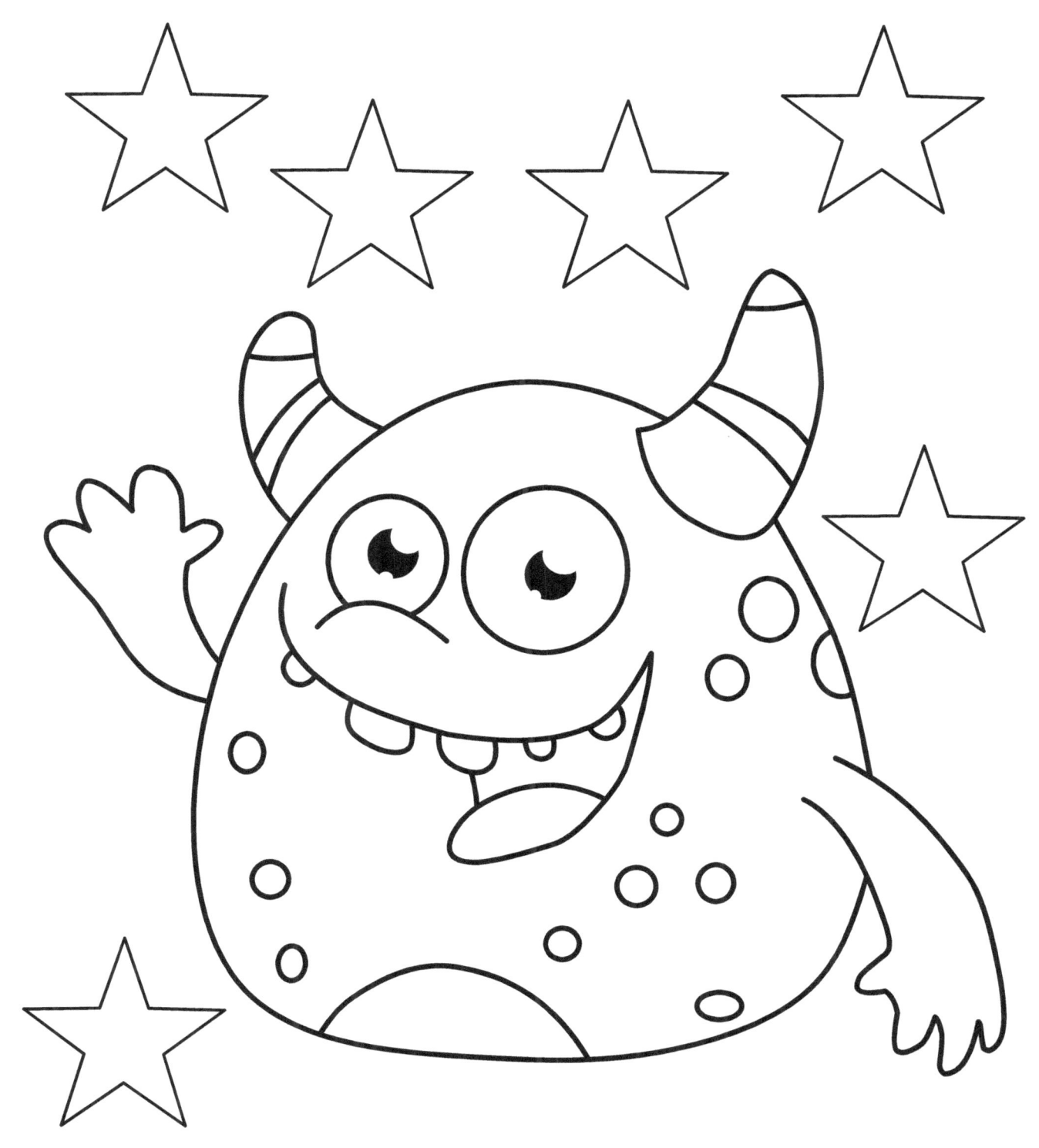

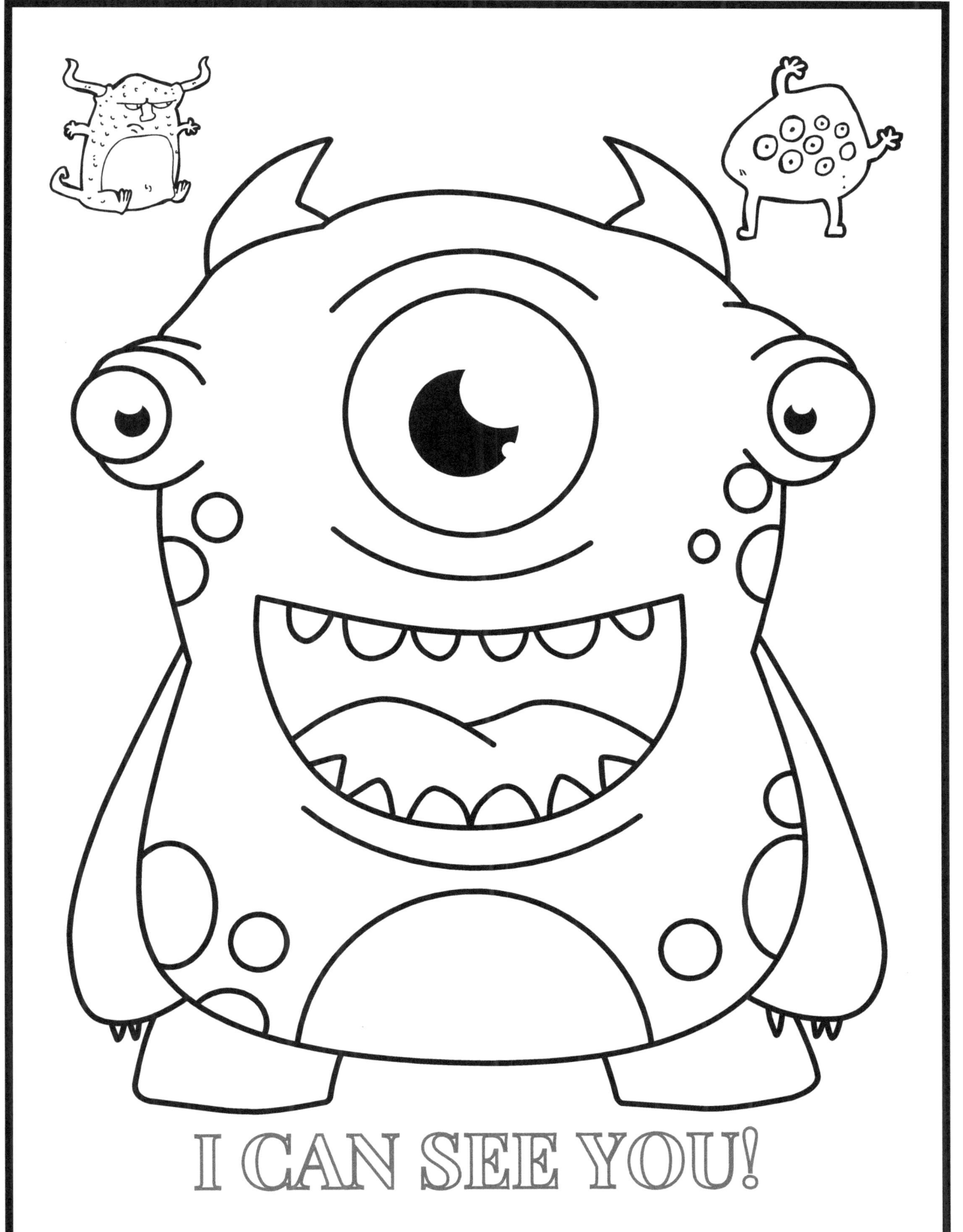

SITTING ON THE GRASS

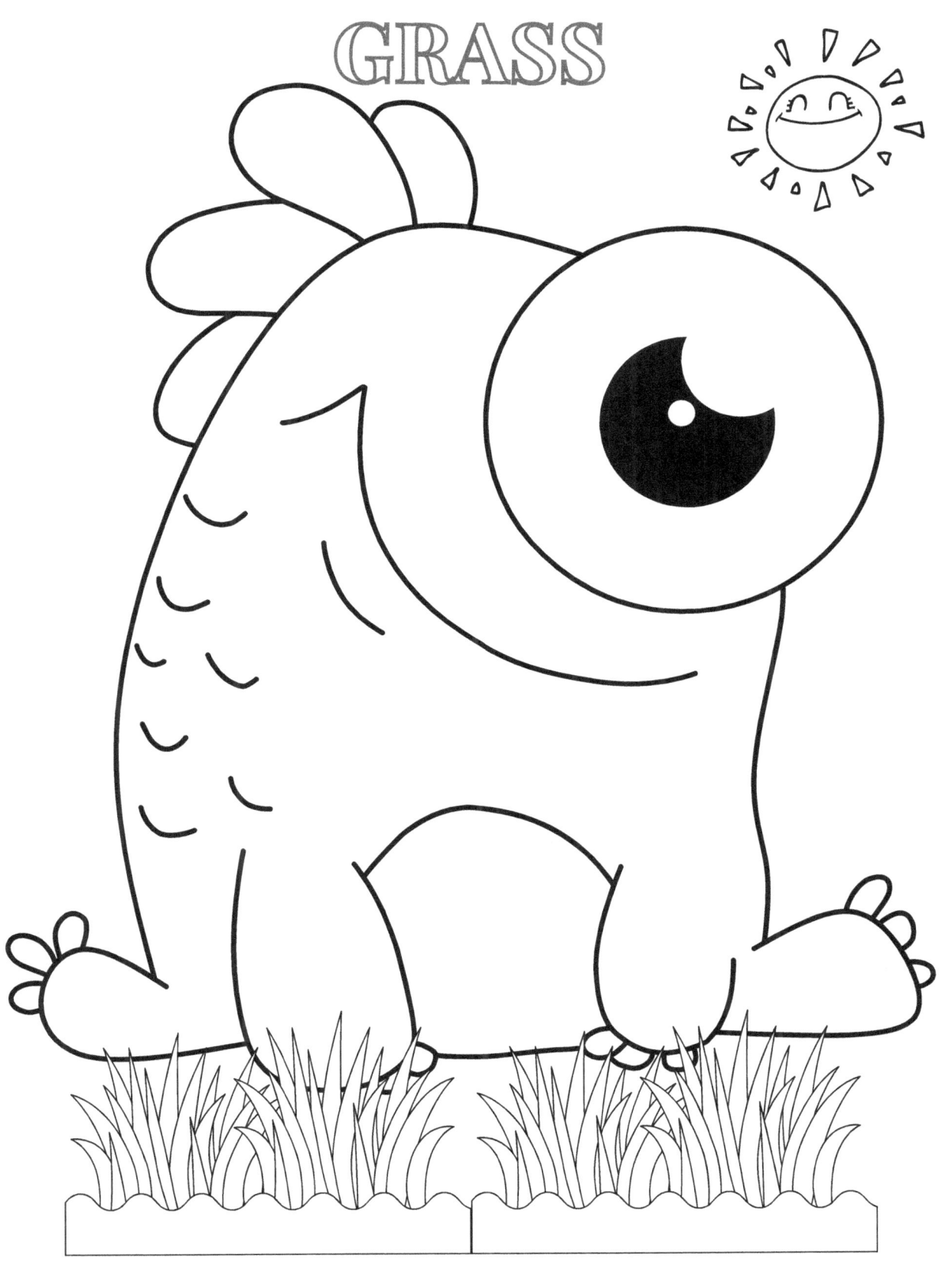

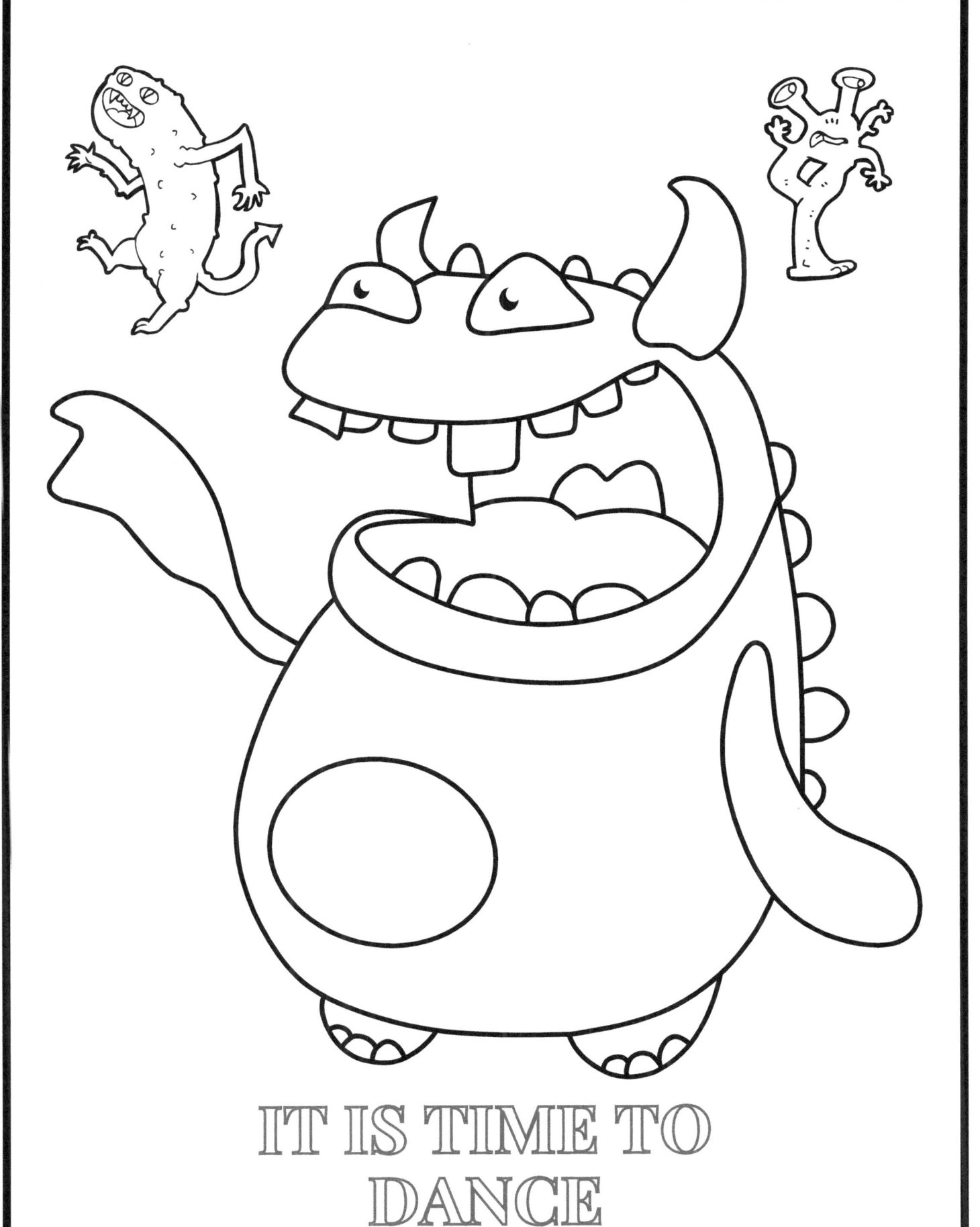

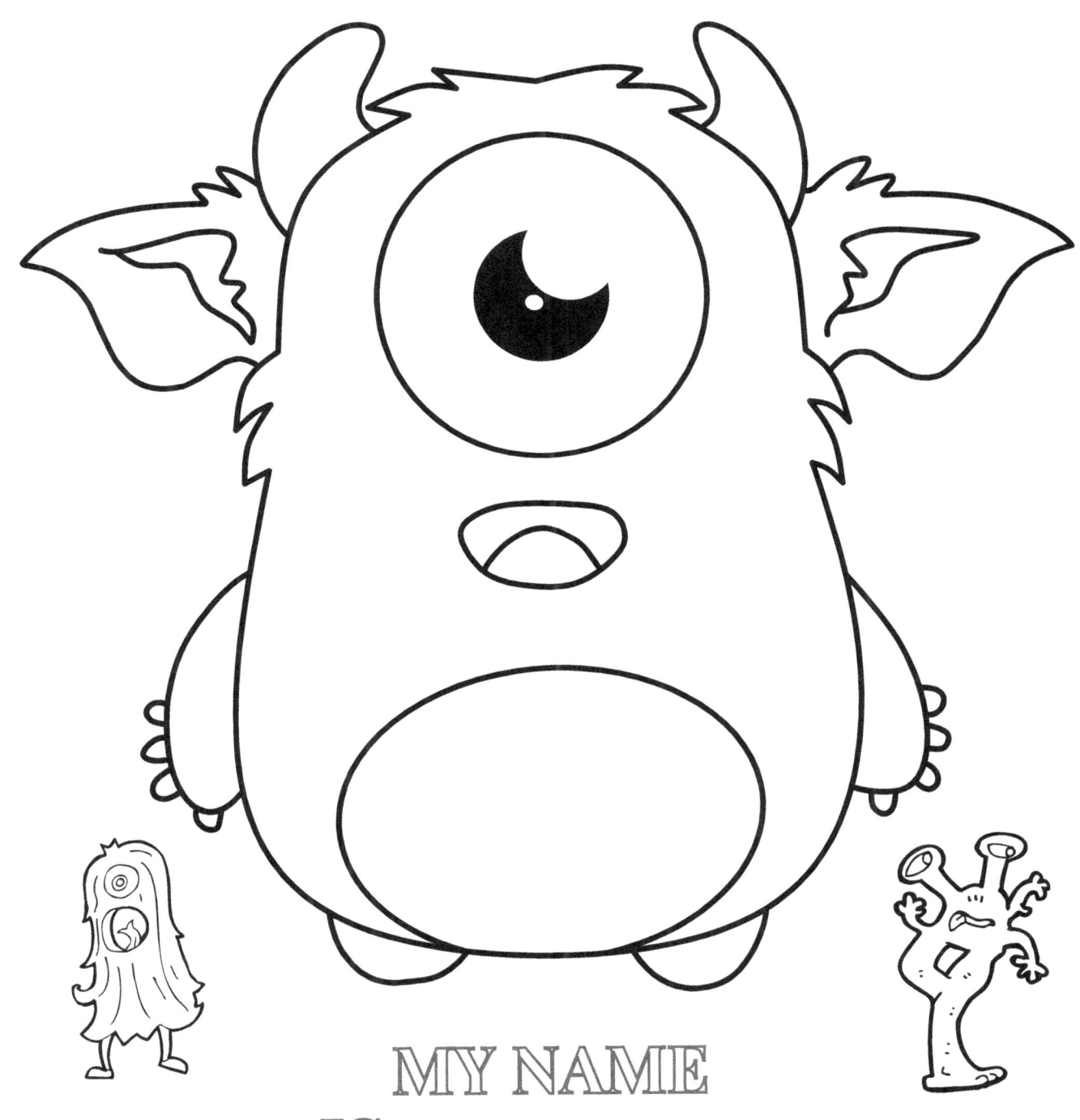

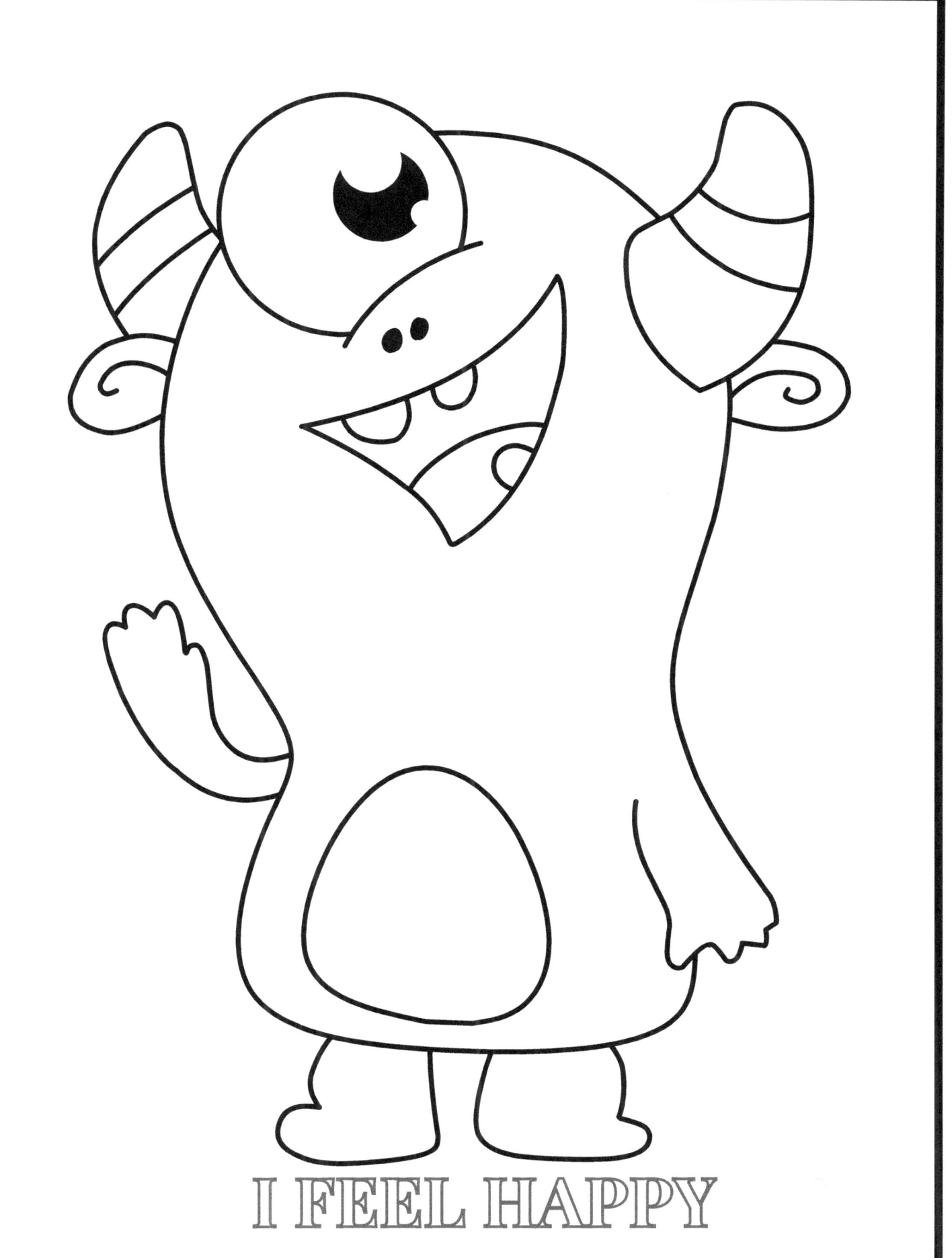

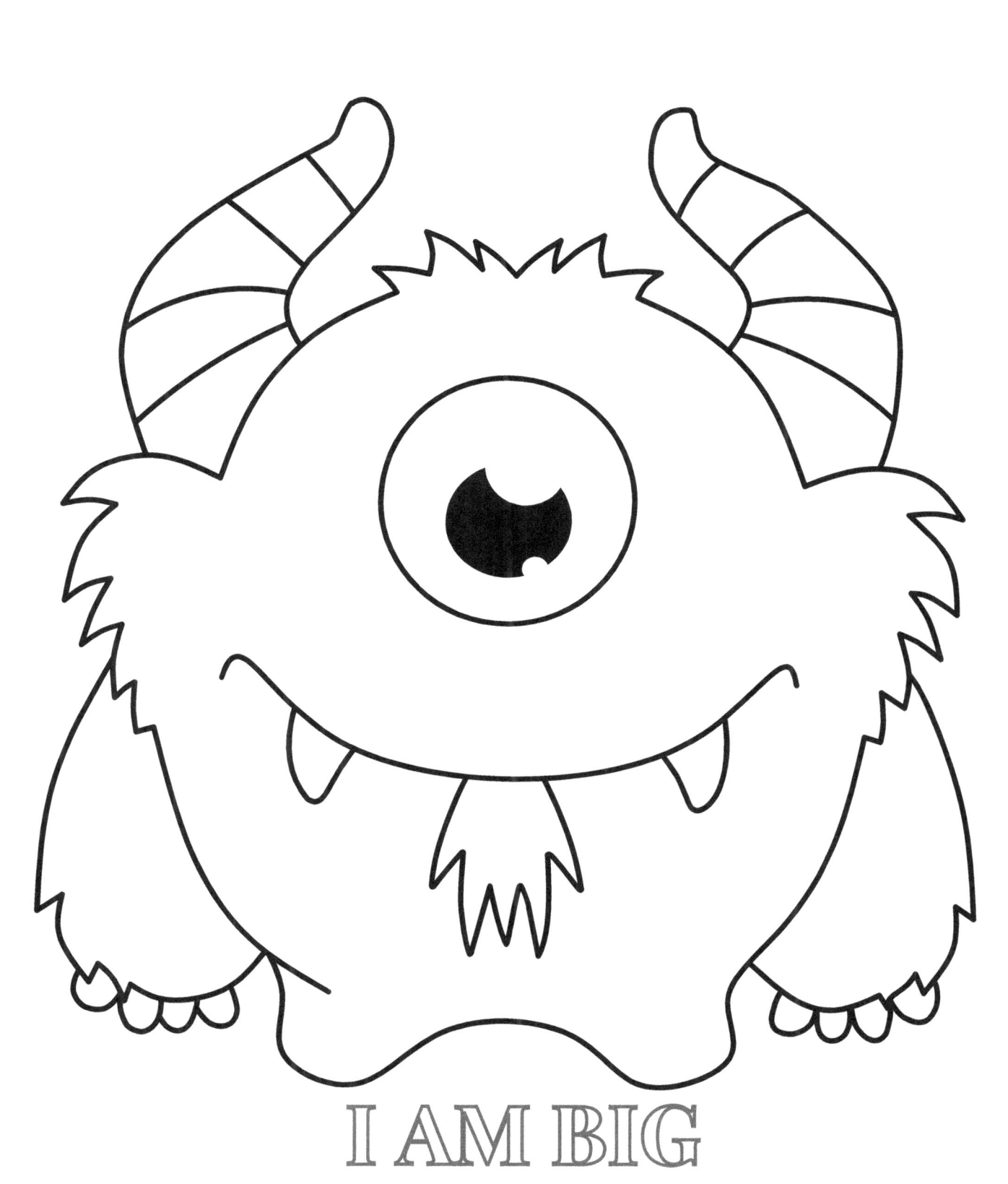

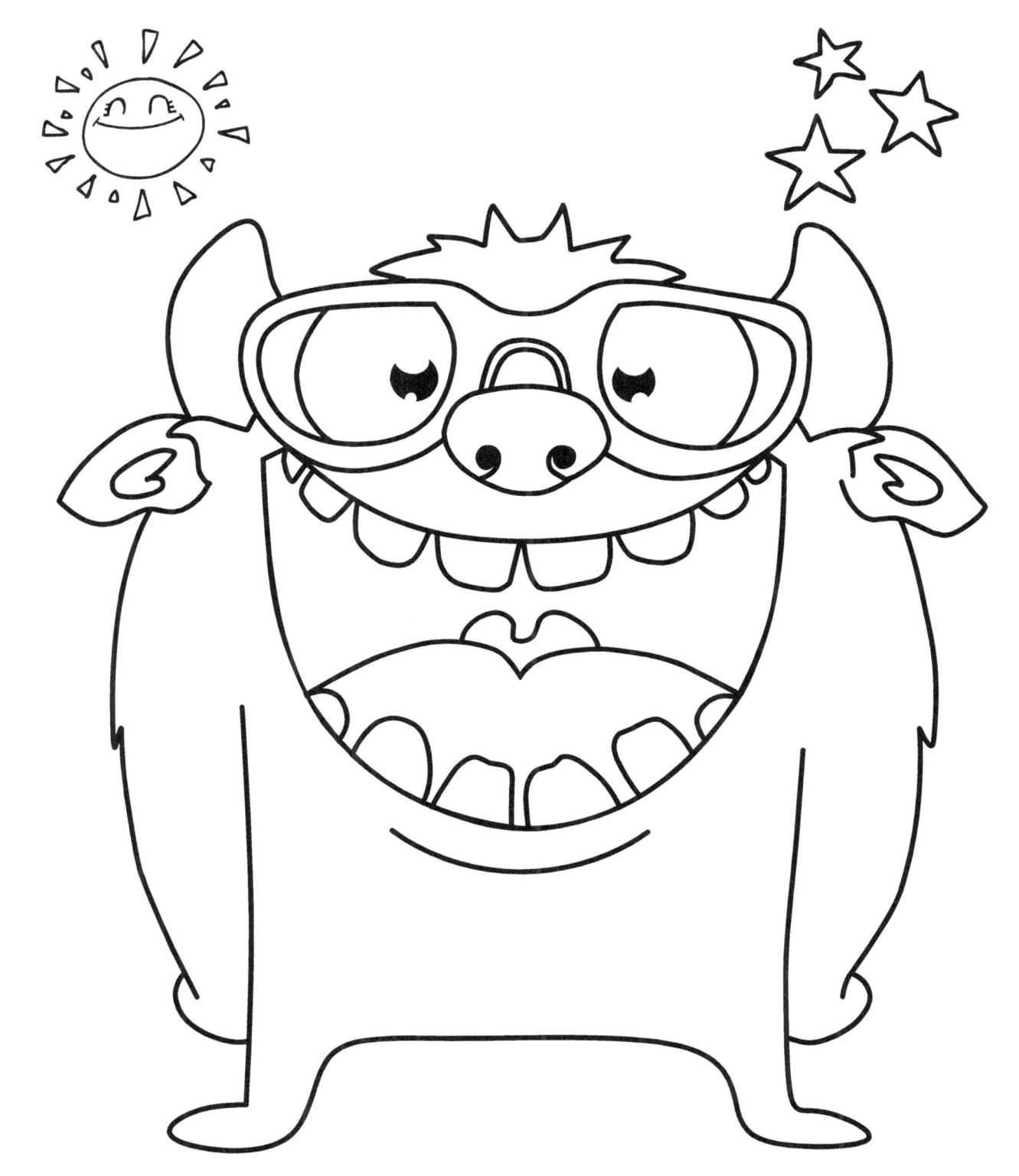

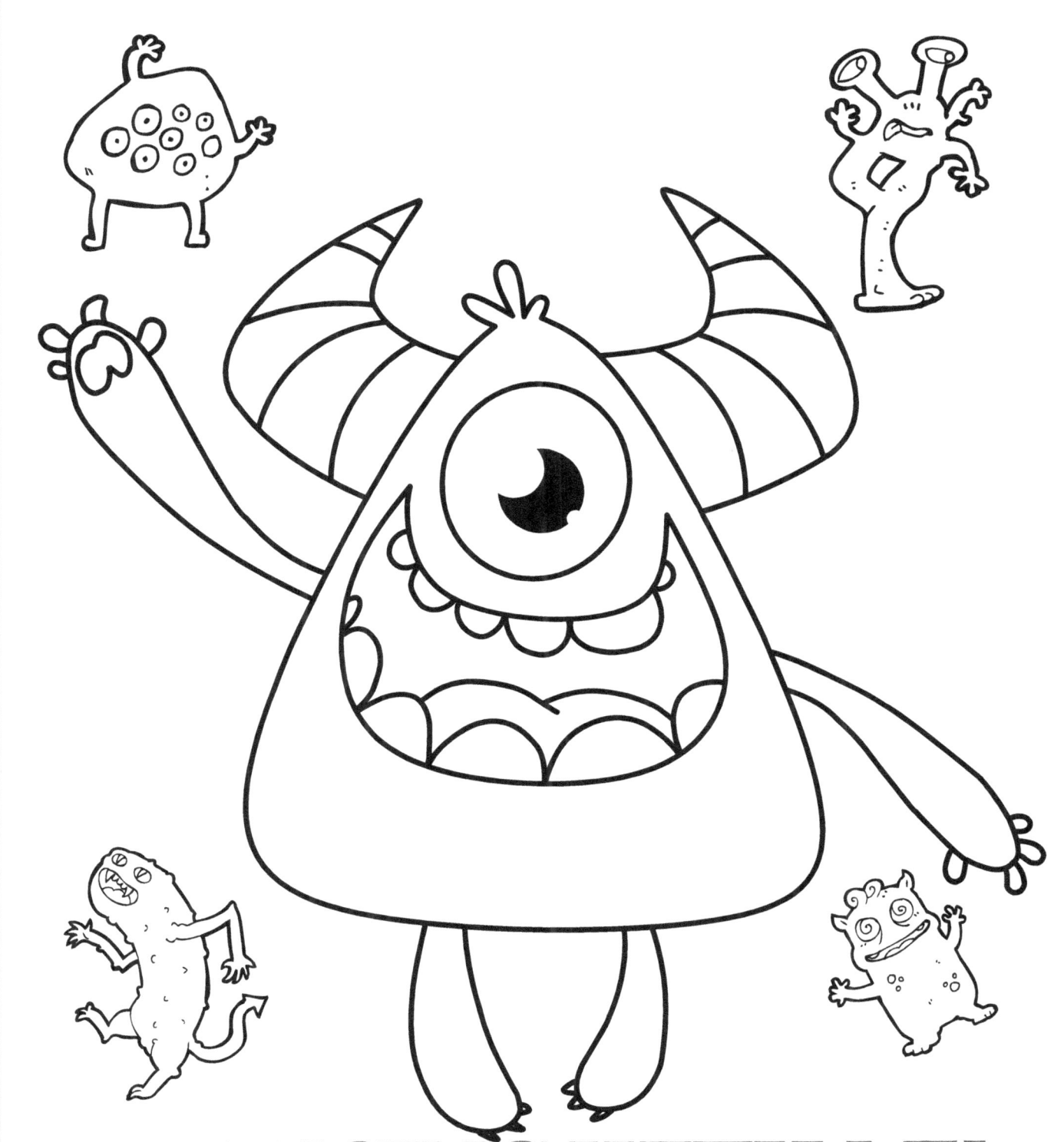

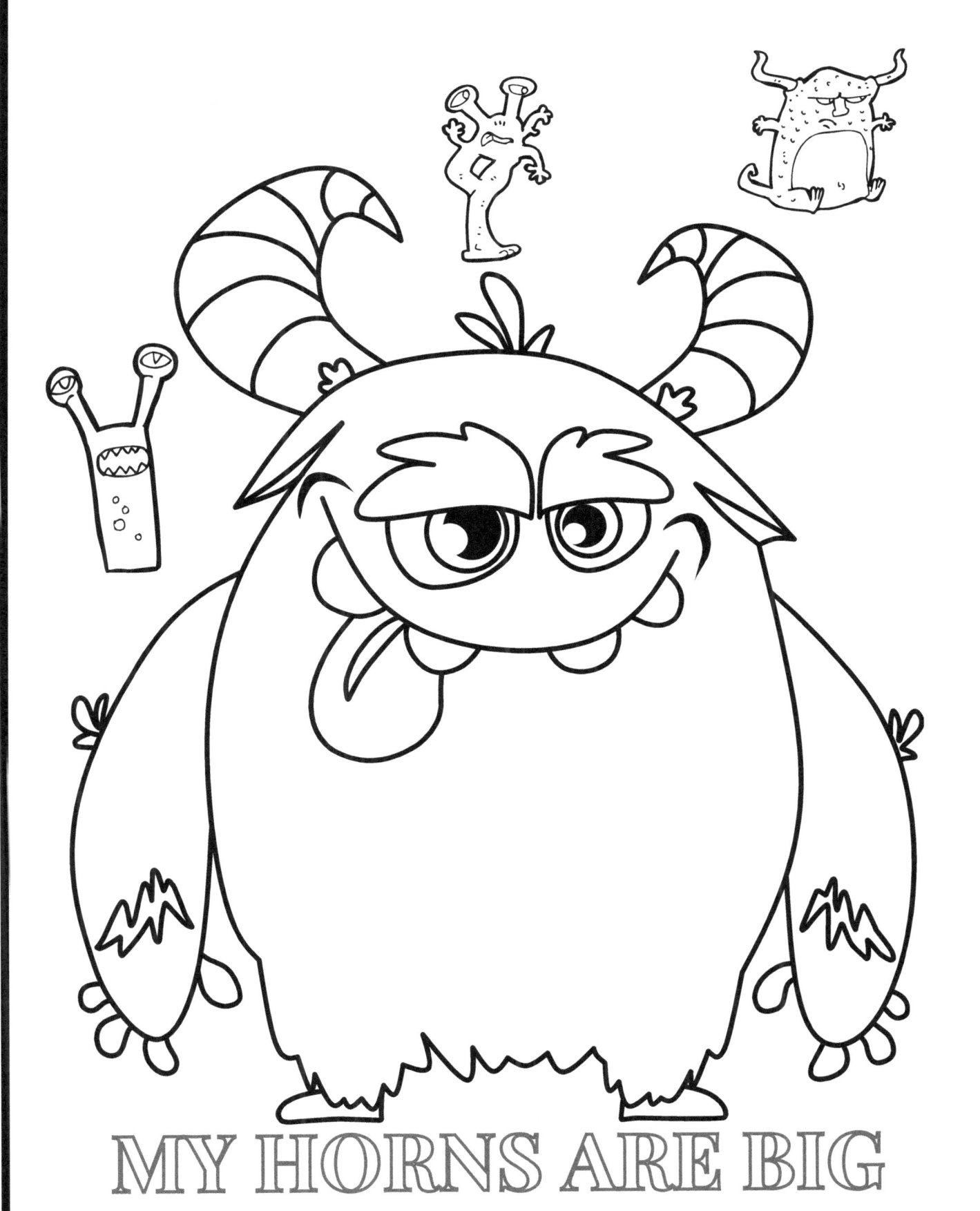

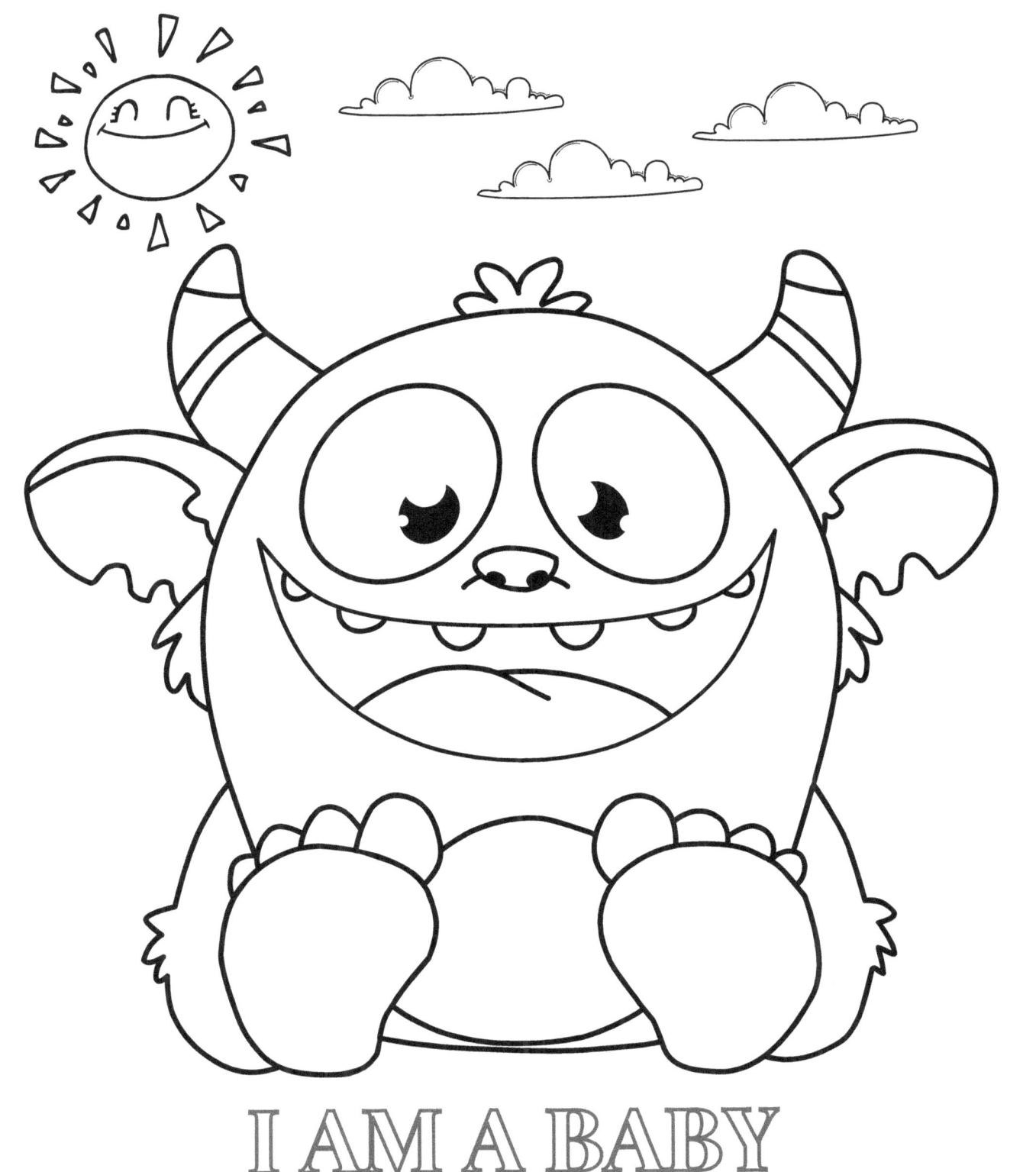

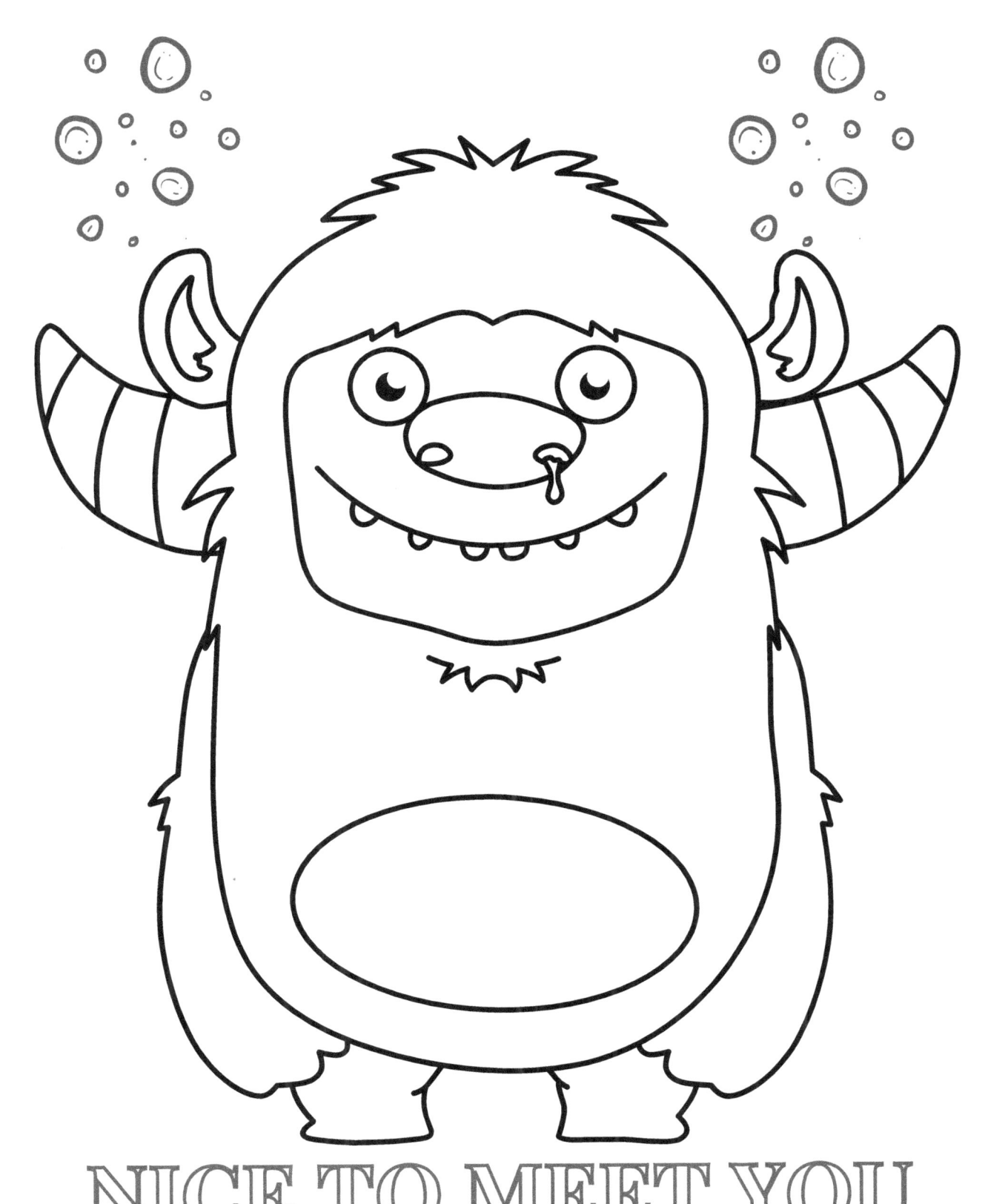

www.ingramcontent.com/pod-product-compliance
Lightning Source LLC
Chambersburg PA
CBHW080904220526
45466CB00011BA/3464